T0036356

ORDINARY
PEOPLE
CHANGE
— THE —
WORLD

I am Dolly Parton

BRAD MELTZER

illustrated by Christopher Eliopoulos

 DIAL BOOKS FOR YOUNG READERS

I am **DOLLY PARTON.**

Once upon a time, on the coldest day of the year in the foothills of the Great Smoky Mountains of East Tennessee, a little girl was born in a one-room cabin.

That girl was me!

If that sounds like a fairy tale, you'll see . . . my life sure does feel like one.

We were so poor, my daddy paid Dr. Thomas with a sack of cornmeal. I like to joke I've been raking in the dough ever since.

I was the fourth of twelve kids, a little firecracker unafraid to wrestle with my brothers.

Eventually, we moved to a two-room shack.

For all of us!

Growing up, my momma read me stories from the Bible, which planted the seeds for my love of reading. One of my favorite books was this one, *The Little Engine That Could.*

Books showed me there was a world beyond the Smoky Mountains.

As kids, to keep the wind out, we'd use newspapers as wallpaper.

It may sound strange, but it was fun to stand on our heads and read the comics.

I'll tell you one thing about being poor: It makes you creative. To save money, my daddy would carve wood toys, while my momma would make us dolls outta corncobs.

The only time we all got store-bought toys was Christmas—one toy for each of us.

My brothers would get fireworks.

I'd get a doll—it didn't even have clothes, but I thought it was so fancy.

One Christmas, Daddy told us he wasn't buying any presents.

He needed the money to finally get my momma a real wedding ring.

That year, our Christmas present was a single box of chocolate-covered cherries that we all shared.

DON'T FEEL BAD.

SEEING MY MOMMA HAPPY MADE IT THE MOST SPECIAL CHRISTMAS OF ALL.

Y'see, to understand who I am, you need to understand where I'm from—and also *who* I come from.

My daddy taught me the value of hard work.

But it was my momma's side that gave me the gift of music.

Today, it's easy to find music on the TV or radio.

But back then, we didn't have electricity.

Luckily, we did lots of singin' in church.

THERE YOU GO, DOLLY— JUST LIKE THAT.

Some said my voice was weird. But I kept singing.

Even before I could write, I was making up songs.
To stand out, since Daddy didn't let us wear makeup,
I'd put flour on my face and rouge my cheeks with pokeberries.

My first "performances" were on our porch, with a tin can for a microphone.
I'd sing to the kids I was babysitting.

I'd sing to whatever animals I could find.

Heck, I'd sing to dirt
if no one was around.

When I was ten years old, my uncle Bill got me my first radio performance.

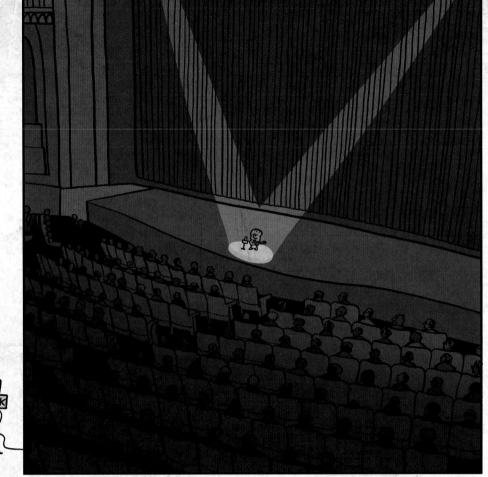

I looked for help. But I knew it was up to me.

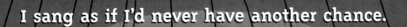

I sang as if I'd never have another chance.

The crowd exploded. And unlike the kids I babysat, none of 'em crawled away.

But if my family taught me anything, it's that success doesn't come easy.

God gives us all our own gifts, but you need hard work to make the most of them.

One fall, my momma made me a patchwork coat outta scraps of fabric.

EVER HEARD THE BIBLE STORY OF JOSEPH AND HIS COAT OF MANY COLORS?

IT WAS GIVEN TO HIM SO HE'D FEEL LOVED AND SPECIAL.

ALMOST DONE?

NOT MUCH LONGER.

When it was finished, I was so excited to show off my coat at school.

I thought it was the grandest thing in the world.

But when other kids saw it...

It's hard when you don't feel like you belong.
So often as a kid, I felt *different*, lonely.
Like I wasn't the same as anyone else.
Where I came from, people never dreamed of seeing the world.
But I wanted to know what was on the other side of the mountain.

It's why I love butterflies so much. I used to imagine that they had a magic powder that'd let me fly and see the world.

I know that makes me sound like a dreamer. But that's a good thing.

You never know where your dreams can take you.
At twelve years old, mine took me to an abandoned
nearby church that I went to for some quiet time.

Inside, I couldn't believe
what I saw.
It wasn't just the old piano.
It was something else.
Something I could feel.

Like God was shining a light
and wanted me to be me.
Like it was all right for me
to dream.
All right for me to see the world.
And of course...

All right for me to sing my songs.
At thirteen, I got on a big interstate bus with my grandma.
My uncle said if I could get to Lake Charles, Louisiana,
I'd get my very own recording session.
I'd never traveled like this.

And boy . . .

That same year, I got to sing at the Grand Ole Opry,
where the most famous country music singers perform.
A musician named Johnny Cash introduced me.

I got called back for three encores.

At my high school graduation, each student was asked to announce their plans for the future.
I told everyone...

I'M GOING TO NASHVILLE TO BECOME A STAR!

The crowd laughed.
It made me even more determined.

The very next morning, I was on a bus to Nashville. I had my dreams, an old guitar, and matching luggage: three paper bags from the grocery store.

Most important, I had my songs.
I'd write songs everywhere: on napkins, torn paper, even on Kleenex boxes.
Sometimes, I'd write while on the bus.
And sure, I wrote about love and heartbreak, like other country singers.
But I also wrote about things that were more personal.

My music career felt like it was finally starting.

After winning an award for Country Song of the Year,
I got an offer to be the co-host of a popular TV show.

Even there, I kept writing songs, especially about subjects that were
overlooked by others—problems that everyday people went through.

But lemme tell ya, the more successful I became, the more some people tried to treat me like a sidekick. I'm nobody's sidekick.

I THINK IT'S TIME FOR ME TO LEAVE THE SHOW AND GO OUT ON MY OWN.

YOU'RE GONNA REGRET THIS.

I didn't regret it. My co-host made me pay him around one million dollars, saying he was the reason for my success.

I knew he was wrong, and that it would take me years to get that money back.

We eventually made up—forgiveness is vital—but I wanted a fresh start, and I knew with hard work, I'd make it on my own.

That's exactly what happened.
Instead of wearing what other people wanted me to wear,
I put on flashy, colorful costumes that fit my personality.

Instead of just singing country songs, I started singing to all audiences.

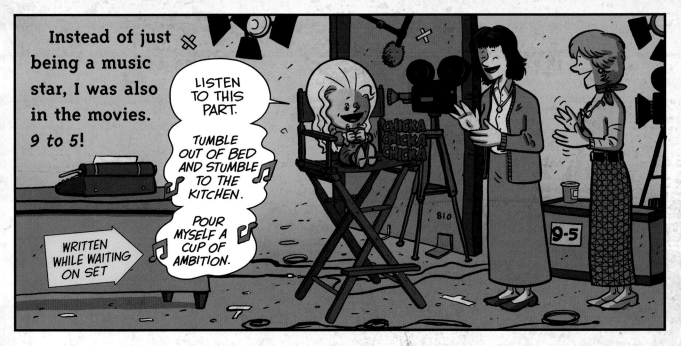

Instead of just being a music star, I was also in the movies. *9 to 5!*

WRITTEN WHILE WAITING ON SET

LISTEN TO THIS PART.

TUMBLE OUT OF BED AND STUMBLE TO THE KITCHEN.

POUR MYSELF A CUP OF AMBITION.

I even started my own charity—Dolly Parton's Imagination Library— which promotes reading by giving away free books to kids like you. The first book we started with? *The Little Engine That Could.*

READING AND EDUCATION IS HOW YOU HELP KIDS FIND THEIR HAPPILY EVER AFTER.

In every song I sing, know what I'm really doing?
Telling a story.
Stories of everyday people.
Poor people.
People who feel invisible
or unseen.

I write about women and men going through the hard parts of life. And the more I sing about triumphs and sorrows, the more people realize they aren't alone.

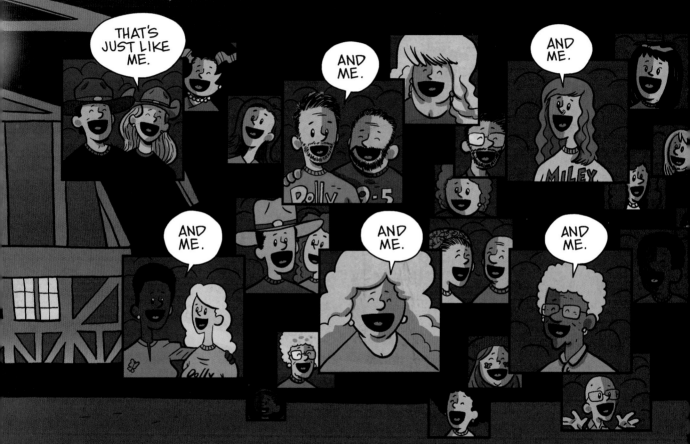

At my concerts, you can find the old and young, rich and poor, gay and straight, city folks and country folks, Black and white, and everyone else you can imagine.

I love 'em all.

I don't judge who people are as long as they're themselves.

In my life, I came from humble beginnings—
and that was just fine by me.
I was never ashamed of it.
It made me who I am.
And it gave me the foundations of my life:
my faith, my family, and my music.

It's okay to be different.
It's okay to feel unseen.
Sometimes the world won't be cheering for you.
But *I* will be.

Whatever mountain gets in your path,
keep climbing . . .

There's only one thing you gotta be in life: Yourself.
Whatever you are, be authentically that.
And the people who look, sound, or think different from you?
Love them for who they are too.

Your dreams are worth dreaming.
Your songs are worth singing.
Your story is worth telling.
Just as it is.
Be proud of who you are,
and don't ever limit yourself.

I am Dolly Parton,
and I see the light that
shines within you.

"The way I see it, if you want the rainbow, you gotta put up with the rain!"

—DOLLY PARTON

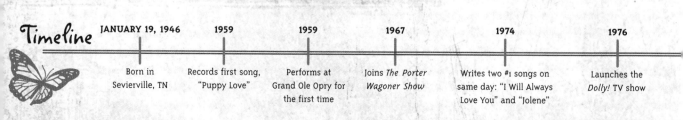

Timeline

JANUARY 19, 1946	1959	1959	1967	1974	1976
Born in Sevierville, TN	Records first song, "Puppy Love"	Performs at Grand Ole Opry for the first time	Joins *The Porter Wagoner Show*	Writes two #1 songs on same day: "I Will Always Love You" and "Jolene"	Launches the *Dolly!* TV show

Dolly as a child

At Dollywood

Reading an Imagination Library selection

Dolly on the stage, 2011

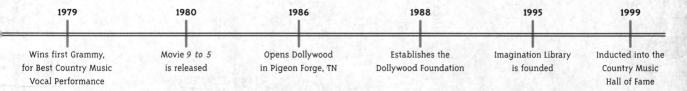

1979	1980	1986	1988	1995	1999
Wins first Grammy, for Best Country Music Vocal Performance	Movie 9 to 5 is released	Opens Dollywood in Pigeon Forge, TN	Establishes the Dollywood Foundation	Imagination Library is founded	Inducted into the Country Music Hall of Fame

For Uncle Richie,
who always followed the song in his heart,
forever excited to see what was on the other
side of the mountain
—B.M.

For Chris DeMaio,
a kind person with a good soul
—C.E.

For historical accuracy, we used Dolly Parton's actual dialogue and lyrics whenever possible. For more of her true voice, we recommend and acknowledge the below titles. Special thanks to the inspiring and incredible Dolly Parton as well as the generous David Dotson and all our friends at the Dollywood Foundation for their input on early drafts.

· ·

SOURCES

Dolly: My Life and Other Unfinished Business by Dolly Parton (HarperCollins, 1994)

Dolly on Dolly: Interviews and Encounters with Dolly Parton (Musicians in Their Own Words) edited by Randy L. Schmidt
(Chicago Review, 2017)

She Come By It Natural: Dolly Parton and the Women Who Lived Her Songs
by Sarah Smarsh (Scribner, 2020)

Dolly Parton, Songteller: My Life in Lyrics by Dolly Parton with Robert K. Oermann
(Chronicle, 2020)

FURTHER READING FOR KIDS

Who Is Dolly Parton? by True Kelley (Penguin Workshop, 2014)

The Little Engine That Could by Wally Piper (Grosset & Dunlap, 2001)

Coat of Many Colors by Dolly Parton (Grosset & Dunlap, 2016)

· ·

DIAL BOOKS FOR YOUNG READERS
An imprint of Penguin Random House LLC, New York

First published in the United States of America by Dial Books for Young Readers, an imprint of Penguin Random House LLC, 2022
Text copyright © 2022 by Forty-four Steps, Inc. • Illustrations copyright © 2022 by Christopher Eliopoulos

Dial and colophon are registered trademarks of Penguin Random House LLC.

Visit us online at penguinrandomhouse.com.

Penguin supports copyright. Copyright fuels creativity, encourages diverse voices, promotes free speech, and creates a vibrant culture. Thank you for buying an authorized edition of this book and for complying with copyright laws by not reproducing, scanning, or distributing any part of it in any form without permission. You are supporting writers and allowing Penguin to continue to publish books for every reader.

Library of Congress Cataloging-in-Publication Data is available.

Photo on page 38 by Valerie Macon courtesy of Getty Images Entertainment. Dollywood photo on page 39 by Ron Davis courtesy of Archive Photos/Getty Images. Dolly in pink on page 39 courtesy of WENN Rights Ltd/Alamy Stock Photo. Photos on page 39 of Dolly as a child and Dolly reading to children courtesy of the Dollywood Foundation.

ISBN 9780593405925 • Printed in the United States of America • 10 9 8 7 6 5 4 3 2 1
PC
Designed by Jason Henry • Text set in Triplex • The artwork for this book was created digitally.